The Book of Wisdom, Rhymes, and Wizardry

Books Available By Dan Clark:

Forgotten Fundamentals—The Answers Are in the Box
Best or Right—Why Great Is Not Good Enough
Chicken Soup for the College Soul
Puppies for Sale and Other Inspirational Tales
Puppies for Sale (Illustrated Storybook)
Clark's Children's Classics
Soul Food, Volumes I and II (The Collection)
The Funniest Things Happen When You Look for Laughs
The Thrill of Teaching
Rainbows Follow Rain
Lyrical Poetry
Privilege of the Platform—The Art and Science of Public Speaking
Only the Best on Leadership
Only the Best on Customer Service

Order at his web site: www.danclarkspeak.com

The Book of
Wisdom, Rhymes, and Wizardry

by *New York Times* Best-Selling Author

Dan Clark

CFI

Springville, Utah

ISBN 13: 978-1-59955-049-7

Published by CFI, an imprint of Cedar Fort, Inc., 2373 W. 700 S., Springville, UT, 84663
Distributed by Cedar Fort, Inc., www.cedarfort.com

Cover design by Nicole Williams

Printed in the United States of America

10 9 8 7 6 5 4 3 2 1

Printed on acid-free paper

CONTENTS

ACKNOWLEDGMENTS

For my special teachers who believed in me when others wouldn't: Ms. Dubois, Mrs. Inman, Dr. Morray, Mrs. Smart, Principal Richards, Mr. Croft, Mr. Thorem, and Coaches Din Morris, Brooks, Allen, Wageman, Trost, Martin, Weight, Simons, Banker, Zimmer, McBride, and Gadd.

For Russ Anderson, Don Pugh, Doug Miller, Fran Peak, Dick Nourse, Zig Ziglar, Jim and Karen Koeninger, Norm Gibbons, Lila Bjorkland, Micky Fisher, Jennifer Lapine, Ernie Wilhoit, Don Wilson, Kay Baker, Pat Mutch, Steve Cosgrove, Les Hewitt, Don Gale, Michael Gale, Chuck Coonradt, Charles Reid, Steve Munn, Wayne and Ruby Clark, Paul Clark, Kelly Clark, Gen. Hal Hornburg (Ret.), Maj. Gen. Johnny Weida, and Laura Calchera (Supreme Commander) for helping me launch my career and/or take it to the next level.

For my National Speakers Association inspiration: Mark Victor Hansen, Jack Canfield, Gail Larsen, Naomi Rhode, Dave Gordon, Robert Henry, Renee Strom, Keith Harrell, Roger Crawford, Bubba Bechtol, Grady Jim Robinson, Jim Tunney, Jeanne Robertson, Bob Murphy, Patricia Fripp, Ray Pelletier, Max Dixon, Mark Sanborn, and Art Berg.

For Bill Kimball, Bob and Paul Mendenhall, Dick Clissold, Bill Gibbs, Jay Jensen, Bob Raybould, Lincoln Hanks, President Royden and Sister Derrick, Phillip Gibson, Mark Tuttle, Gary Mangum, Scott Buie, Mark Monsen, Mont Beardall, Blain Hope, Todd Petersen, Colin and Theresa Dunne, Brendan and Evelyn Gibley, Todd Morgan, Brad Morris, and Brent Bowen for your spirituality, commitment to obedience, faith, and influence in my Christian walk with God.

For K.C., Danny, Nikola, McCall, and Alexandrea for finding wisdom, comfort, laughter, and solace in my speeches, stories, anecdotes, and words. I love you and need you in my life forever.

FOREWORD

My fascination for *Wisdom, Rhymes, and Wizardry* was created and nurtured by my dear, sweet mother, Ruby Clark. Throughout my life she has given me a variety of quotable quotes.

In song writing, you take an entire story and consolidate it to three and a half minutes. The "hook" of a catchy chorus line is what makes it a hit. Some examples are "Thank God for unanswered prayers" and "It was the sickness that made me well."

In a joke, the punch line makes the entire joke funny: "During a test a kid whispers, 'How close are you to the answer?' His friend replies, 'Two seats away!' "

In sports, coaches inspire with these same catchy quotes. My own coaches inspired me to reflect on life and to create my own memorable quotes. There is no better way to communicate quickly, powerfully, and directly than through short golden nuggets of wisdom that you can "hang your hat on" or "put in your pipe and smoke."

Brian Piccalo said, "You can't quit; it's a league rule."

Steve Marlowe said, "Sportsmanship is when an athlete walks off the field . . . and you can't tell whether he has won or lost. His hushed dignity, respect for the game, and knowledge that he left it all on the field let him stand tall and be proud."

Bear Bryant said, "If a player is going to quit, I want him to quit at practice, not during a game. That's why I make practice so hard."

Tom Gadd said, "Practice doesn't make perfect; it makes permanent. Perfect practice makes perfect."

I say, "Every play, every day, there's always a way. Find it!"

Is life easy or hard? No one said it would be easy. They only said it would be worth it. Success is hard. The hard is what makes it great.

If it was easy, everybody would achieve it.

What is life all about? Society continually bombards us with commands to balance our lives, make more money, manage our time, and peak our performance, so to whom do we turn to get the job done? Turn to a wizard.

Wizards are essentially mentors, but the title "mentor" sounds academic and sterile. Mentors enforce the letter of the law. Mentors see with eyesight, but wizards see with insight. The title "wizard" encompasses magic and passion. Wizards are emotional and enforce the spirit of the law. Wizards use creativity and imagination to cut through the clutter of daily life to reveal the wisdom, rhymes, and wizardry that empower us. I present some of my favorites here so that you may internally excavate life's littlest lessons and emerge as an artist of being fully alive. Enjoy!

LEADERSHIP

Standing in the front of a room and calling yourself a leader does not make you a leader any more than standing in the middle of a garage makes you a truck. Leading others begins when we lead and grow ourselves and become lifelong learners. Remember:

Learners retain:

- 10 percent of what they read;
- 20 percent of what they hear;
- 30 percent of what they see;
- 50 percent of what they see and hear;
- 70 percent of what they write and say;
- 90 percent of what they write, say, and do.

Stop, look, listen, copy it down, share it, and do it!

We must teach correct principles and empower others to govern themselves. It's what we do when the leader is not around that makes us champions.

* ✶ *

Leadership is an analog job in a digital world. Leaders have courage to adjust mistakes, vision to welcome change, and confidence to stay out of step when everyone else is marching to the wrong tune. The purpose of leaders is to breed more leaders. We rise higher and see farther when we stand on the strong shoulders of those who have gone before us and those who continually support us and follow our lead.

Life is not measured by the number of breaths we take, but by the number of moments that take our breath away. We do not remember days; we remember moments.

* * *

A celebrity is a big name; a hero is a big person. The masses define celebrities, but heroes define themselves. Heroes are successful because they are willing to do what others are not willing to do. They do not want to do the hard things in life, either, but they do them anyway. They understand that courage is the mastery—not the absence—of fear.

PERSPECTIVE

The main thing
is to make
the main thing
the main thing.

* * *

Some things are true whether you believe them or not. Everybody is entitled to their own opinion, but nobody is entitled to the wrong facts. Fact: we should not major in minor things or get caught up in the thick of thin things.

You will become a champion only when losing hurts worse than winning feels good.

* * *

You cannot discipline the wrong person to do the right thing. There is no right way to do something wrong.

* * *

You must learn to do something exactly right slowly, before you can learn to do it exactly right quickly.

Don't get discouraged; it is often the last key in the bunch that opens the lock.

⁎ ✶ ⁎

The early bird gets the worm, but the second mouse gets the cheese.

⁎ ✶ ⁎

It's easier to act your way into positive thinking than to think your way into positive action. It's not mind over matter, but matter over mind. Action is what creates the good feeling.

The only thing you are not in charge of is whether you are in charge.

* * *

When your attitude is right, your abilities will always catch up.

* * *

Pressure is not naturally there. It's created when you question your own ability. When you know what you can do, there is never any question.

The mind once stretched can never return to its original dimensions.

* * *

You must stretch before you can strengthen, and all the strengthening occurs in the area past the point of discomfort.

* * *

There is a giant difference between inspiration and motivation. Inspiration affects attitude—the way we think. Motivation affects behavior—the way we act. No one person can motivate another person. We can only inspire others to want to motivate themselves. True motivation comes from within.

What you are afraid to do is a clear indicator of the next thing you need to do. The things you hate to hear the most are usually the things you need to hear the most.

* ✶ *

Everyone dies, but not everyone truly lives. Dream big. When you lose your dreams, you die. So many people walk dead through the halls of life, and they don't even know it.

Dreams come one or two sizes too big so we can grow into them.

⁎ ✶ ⁎

If you don't have a dream, how are you going to make a dream come true?

⁎ ✶ ⁎

Circumstances never destroy dreams. Dreams live in your mind and heart. Only there can they die.

You are the message. Some people would rather be popular for the moment than respected for a lifetime. Popularity is other people liking you. Happiness is you liking yourself.

* * *

Our business in life is not to get ahead of others, but to get ahead of ourselves—to break our own records and to improve our tomorrow through the lessons of yesterday and the actions of today.

* * *

Life is not measured by the number of breaths we take, but by the number of moments that take our breath away. We do not remember days, we remember moments.

Start by doing what's necessary; then do what's possible, and suddenly you are doing the impossible.

* * *

We don't learn to *know,* we learn to *do.* It doesn't do us any good to know how to read if we never pick up a book and read it. Learning is a process we can't skip. Doing is a process of proving that it was worth learning.

The illiterate of the future are not those who can't read or write, but those who cannot learn, unlearn, and relearn.

* * *

Quality of life means more than new furniture. The quality of our judgment precisely determines the quality of life. We should not believe everything that we think. Head knowledge is not necessarily true.

AUTHENTICITY

We ultimately have no choice but to feel what we are feeling. Authenticity only comes when we compare ourselves with ourselves. The meaning of success and failure emerges only in comparison to something or someone else. The one-eyed man is king in the land of the blind. Anorexia and bulimia are not eating disorders; they are not behavioral and have nothing to do with food. A young woman alone on an island with no fashion magazines to look at and no one else around to compare herself against would not know if she was tall or short, skinny or overweight. She would simply be her real, beautiful, unique self. She would know that "God don't make no junk!"

The most visible creators are those whose medium is life itself. They express the inexpressible without brush, hammer, clay, or guitar. They neither paint nor sculpt. Their medium is being. Whatever their presence touches increases life. They see, and they don't have to draw. They are the artists of being fully alive.

THE TWELVE PRECEPTS OF BEING FULLY ALIVE

1. *Find a wizard.* You have to stretch before you can strengthen.
2. *Live on purpose.* Where did you come from? Why are you here? Where are you going?
3. *Focus on fundamentals.* Become brilliant at the basics.
4. *Establish mutual respect and support.* Celebrate people's differences.
5. *Find the opportunity in change.* When your horse dies, dismount.
6. *Act "as if."* If you do the thing, you will have the power.
7. *Communicate.* Don't just take turns talking.
8. *Come to grips with death, then life.* We are all going to die—deal with it.
9. *Be true to yourself.* "God don't make no junk."
10. *Keep swinging.* You can't quit; it's a league rule.
11. *Increase feedback.* No matter what your past has been, you have a spotless future.
12. *Follow the final formula.* Success is never final.

Self is not discovered; self is created. What we have been in the past does not make us who we are today. What we hope to become in the future makes us who we are today.

* * *

You don't have to be positive; you just have to be yourself. But being yourself is a choice, so you should be positive.

* * *

Be the very best you that you can possibly be. Be everything there is inside you. You will make a lousy anybody else.

We can do only what we think we can do. We can be only what we think we can be. We can have only what we think we can have. What we do, what we are, and what we have all depend upon what we think.

⁎ ✶ ⁎

We do not stop playing because we are old—we grow old because we stop playing.

⁎ ✶ ⁎

When we identify ourselves in terms of what we do instead of who we are, we become a human *doing* instead of a human *being.*

If you don't know what direction to take, you haven't acknowledged where you are. You have to see what you are and say what you are before you can leave where you are and go where you want to be.

* * *

Love people for where they are in their lives.

* * *

The only place from which people can grow is where they are. We must physically and emotionally go where other people are. Only there can we reach others and invite them to grow.

FAMILY

You spend the first two years of your children's lives teaching them to walk and talk, and you spend the next sixteen years telling them to sit down and shut up.

* * *

Cleaning your house while your kids are still growing is like clearing the driveway before it has stopped snowing.

There is only one pretty child in the world, and every mother has it.

✶ ✶ ✶

Children naturally mimic their parents, despite the parents' every effort to teach their children good manners.

✶ ✶ ✶

Children seldom misquote you. In fact, they usually repeat word-for-word what you shouldn't have said.

Be nice to your kids; they'll choose your nursing home.

⁎ ✶ ⁎

The main purpose of holding parties for your children is to remind yourself that there are children more awful than your own.

⁎ ✶ ⁎

I've learned that regardless of your relationship with your parents, you miss them terribly after they die.

RELATIONSHIPS

When you put a hard-to-catch horse in the same field with an easy-to-catch horse, you usually end up with two hard-to-catch horses. When you put a sick child in the same room with a healthy child, you usually end up with two sick children. To be great, you need to hang out with the great ones!

* * *

When the water in the lake goes up, all the boats rise together.

Misery finds company; then both parties are happy.

⁎ ✶ ⁎

Positive discipline is catching someone doing something right. You can't increase people's performance by making them feel worse. Humiliation immobilizes behavior. There are only twenty-four hours in a day, and we can't do two things at once. If we say yes to the positive instead of worrying about how to say no to the negative, we won't have time to be negative. Our positives will say no for us. Instead of telling others what they can't do, we should focus on the positive and show them what they can do.

A broken clock is right twice a day.

* * *

Never give up on anybody, especially yourself!

* * *

Failure is an event, not a person. In life there are no mistakes, only lessons. Therefore, praise in public and criticize in private.

Don't expect others to listen to your advice while ignoring your example. I'd rather see a sermon than hear one any day. I'd rather you walk with me than merely show me the way.

* * *

If the things we think about are different than the things we do, we will never be happy.

* * *

Use your wit to amuse, not to abuse.

What you say is exactly what you intend to say.

⁂

There are none so righteous as the newly converted.

⁂

Sales is everybody's business. Customer service is not a department—it's an attitude. Customers are not outsiders, but a part of the company. Customers do not interrupt the company's work; they are the purpose for it.

Sales and customer service cannot be taught and trained. It's a natural way of thinking and living—a natural tendency and desire to make everybody else around us better. Classic sales and service people strive to bring out the best in everyone. They are everywhere from Michael Jordan, Larry Bird, and Tiger Woods, to an incredible boss, an inspiring spouse, and a best friend.

* ✶ *

Teaching is the profession that makes all other professions possible. Educators are the smartest people on earth. They could work for any major corporation, yet they choose to teach. Thank a teacher, support all teachers, and be a teacher.

* ✶ *

Good, effective communication is more than two people taking turns talking. Stop, make eye contact, understand, and respond. Don't just hear—listen!

VISION

Imagination is the strongest nation on earth.

* * *

The mountain seems high only from the valley.

* * *

Your enemies might become your friends if you allow them to be who they are.

When we set high expectations and work hard to meet them, we call it accomplishment. We had to come early, study more, and stay late; we had to withstand temptation and take the high road, but it was worth it. However, when we set low expectations and allow our behavior to slide down to meet them, we call it rationalization. Rationalization kills our families, neighborhoods, and schools and can destroy the world. It's better to shoot for the stars and miss than to aim for a pile of manure and hit.

⋆ ✶ ⋆

On top of old Smoky, all covered with snow, I lost my best bird dog by aiming too low!

Being burned out means that you were once lit! To rekindle the flame, focus on purposes instead of just setting goals.

* * *

All the information in the world isn't going to make a person successful. It's like the guy with three PhDs—one in psychology, one in philosophy, and one in sociology. He doesn't have a job, but at least he can explain why!

* * *

The person with big dreams, passion, and desire is more powerful than the person with all the facts.

* * *

We should not drag our dreams down to the level of our income—we should elevate our income up to the level of our dreams.

CHARACTER

Crisis does not make or break a person; it just reveals the true character within.

✶ ✶ ✶

Failure is the opportunity to begin again with more knowledge.

✶ ✶ ✶

Some men have thousands of excuses why they cannot do what they want, when all they need is one reason why they can.

Passion will ensure success, for the desire of the end will point out the means. Desire creates the power. Wherever the mind goes, the energy flows.

* * *

Do the right thing simply because it is the right thing to do.

* * *

Do not let what you cannot do interfere with what you can do.

You've gotta be before you can do.
You've gotta do before you can have.
You've gotta have before you can give.
You've gotta give before you can take.

✶ ✶ ✶

You are not a failure if you don't win; you are a failure if you don't participate. It's better to fail with honor than to succeed by fraud.

✶ ✶ ✶

To endure is greater than to dare—
To tire out hostile fortune,
To be daunted by no difficulty,
To keep heart when all have lost it—
Who can say this is not greatness?

TEAMS AND WINNING

It's not all about *team*. Teams lose.

Whoever said it's not whether you win or lose that counts, probably lost. It's about *winning*.

Whoever said there is no *I* in *team* never played on a team.

It's about winning, and winning has two *I*'s in it!

Independent Individual Preparation: a commitment to character, confidence, consistency, and change.

Interdependent Collaboration: a commitment to contribute and cooperate.

The teams that win have the greatest number of "I" players on them!

We are not paid by the hour just because we are on the team. We are paid for the value we bring to that hour, for productivity and for contributing to a winning team.

✶ ✶ ✶

TEAM—Together Everyone Achieves More, and no one has any more to give.

✶ ✶ ✶

There is nothing more insignificant than the half-time score.

✶ ✶ ✶

You cannot quit; it's a league rule!

✶ ✶ ✶

You don't coach results, you coach behavior.

GOALS

Goals are only an excuse for the game. We play the game in between the goals.

* * *

If you don't like the direction the river is flowing, don't jump in.

* * *

There is no future in any job; the future lies in the person who holds that job.

If you are not training and pushing yourself to your ultimate capacity and maximum potential as a human being, someone else is. When you meet that person, he or she will win.

* * *

Happiness is not in the destination, but in the journey. It's not the sugar that makes the tea sweet; it's the stirring.

Success is a process, not a product. We strive for perfection and enjoy excellence in the process of the journey.

* * *

Success is never final.
Failure is never fatal.
Good enough is neither.
Practice makes permanent.
That's why we never say "never"!

* * *

Half of getting what you want is knowing what you must give up to get it.

If you are not rich, notice how you make yourself poor. We do not live to make money; we make money to fully live.

* * *

Decide to get up thirty minutes earlier than usual in the morning. Do this for a year, and you will add seven and one-half days to your waking world.

CHANGE

When your horse dies, dismount!

* * *

If you're not the lead sled dog, the view doesn't ever change much.

* * *

We must find the opportunity in change.

Pain is a signal to grow, not to suffer. Once we learn the lesson the pain is teaching us, the pain goes away. If we try to avoid it, it won't go away until we confront it.

* ✶ *

Worry comes from the belief you are powerless.

* ✶ *

When you fail more than most even try and then confess, you'll fail your way to success!

If you require someone to change, you require that person to lie to you. Change must always come from within. People do things for their own reasons, not other people's.

⁎ ✶ ⁎

There is no change in the absence of emotion.

⁎ ✶ ⁎

There is truth where there are tears.

⁎ ✶ ⁎

In times of change, learners inherit the earth, while the learned find themselves beautifully equipped to deal with a world that no longer exists.

If you think boundary lines take away your freedom, or if you think rules hold you back, think again.

* * *

A kite rises against—not with—the wind. The string does not hold the kite down; it holds the kite up. If you disagree, let go of the string!

FREE ADVICE

Surround yourself with light; it brightens you and everything you're about.

* * *

It's better to build a fence at the edge of the cliff than to park an ambulance at its base.

* * *

If you do the things you need to do when you need to do them, you will be able to do the things you want to do when you want to do them.

THE TEN COMMITMENTS

1. Count your blessings and write "thank you" notes promptly.
2. Record your parents' laughter. Respect your mom and talk to her often.
3. Be someone's hero, inspiration, and role model.
4. Remember people's names, and respect everyone who works for a living, regardless of their jobs.
5. Don't ever be called out on strikes. Go down swinging, and swing for the fence!
6. If you cut your own firewood, it warms you twice.
7. Never cut what can be untied.
8. Return borrowed vehicles with a full tank of gas.
9. Don't burn bridges; you'll be surprised how many times you have to cross the river.
10. When someone hugs you, let them be the first to let go.

Purchase gas from the neighborhood gas station even if it costs more. Next winter when it's freezing and your car won't start, you'll be glad they know you and want to help.

* * *

Buy whatever kids are selling on card tables in their front yards.

* * *

Buy vegetables from farmers on the side of the highway.

Let people pull in front of you when you're stopped in traffic. And be prepared: those you let in flip you a "peace sign," but those you hold up flip you a "half-a-peace" sign!

* * *

I've learned that you shouldn't go through life with a catcher's mitt on both hands. You need to be able to throw something back.

* * *

Many people will walk in and out of your life, but only true friends will leave foot-prints in your heart.

* * *

Conscience is what hurts so bad when every-thing else feels so good.

To handle yourself, use your head; to handle others, use your heart.

⁂

If a man betrays you once, it is his fault; if he betrays you twice, it is your fault.

⁂

Beautiful young people are accidents of nature, but beautiful old people are works of art.

⁂

I've learned that silent company is often more healing than words of advice.

I've learned that if you want to cheer yourself up, you should try cheering someone else up.

* ✶ *

I've learned that if someone says something unkind about me, I must live so that no one will believe it. We shouldn't let someone else's words or actions change who we are and what we say and do. We need to live so that when people are away from us they say, "I like me best when I'm with you; I want to see you again."

I've learned that you can tell a lot about a man by the way he handles these three things: a rainy day, lost luggage, and tangled Christmas tree lights.

* * *

I've learned that whenever I decide something with kindness, I usually make the right decision.

* * *

I've learned that even when I have pains, I don't have to be one.

I've learned that if you pursue happiness, it will elude you. But if you focus on your family, the needs of others, your work, meeting new people, and doing the very best you can, happiness will find you.

* ✶ *

Remember to hold hands and cherish the moment, for someday that person will not be there.

* ✶ *

We resent in others what we don't like about ourselves. We must be the change we seek in our relationships, at home and at work. When we stop growing, we put others down out of insecurity to make ourselves feel better about who we are. Remember, green things keep growing, but ripe things go rotten.

The best gift you can give a loved one is your time.

⁎ ✶ ⁎

We become like the company we keep.

⁎ ✶ ⁎

If the grass looks greener on the other side, it's time to fertilize!

⁎ ✶ ⁎

There's no lesson in the second kick of a donkey.

People who use themselves up are the happiest.

⁎ ✶ ⁎

You can make a *living* with knowledge, but you can make a *life* with wisdom.

⁎ ✶ ⁎

Good manners will take you where money cannot.

⁎ ✶ ⁎

Those who help others feel good about themselves are always in demand.

⁎ ✶ ⁎

If you have to eat an elephant, take it one bite at a time.

To understand all is to forgive much.

* * *

Sometimes it's more fun to travel than it is to arrive.

* * *

Living with resentment is like nursing yourself with poison and waiting for the other fellow to die.

* * *

How you treat others is not about who they are, but who you are.

* * *

You pretty much find what you're looking for.

DID YOU KNOW . . .

No piece of paper can be folded in half more than seven times.

Donkeys kill more people annually than plane crashes.

You burn more calories sleeping than you do watching television.

American Airlines saved $40,000 in 1987 by eliminating one olive from each salad served in first class.

Venus is the only planet that rotates clockwise.

Apples, not caffeine, are more efficient at waking you up in the morning.

Most dust particles in your house are made of dead skin.

A duck's quack doesn't echo, and no one knows why.

Walt Disney was afraid of mice.

COMMON PHRASES

HIT A SNAG

In American lumber camps, a "snag" is a tree trunk fixed firmly in the bottom of a river, just barely protruding from the surface. These trunks are the bane of a lumberjack's existence. If the workers "hit a snag" while driving logs downstream, the cut timber gets jammed and cannot roll. Workers cannot make progress until they remove the snag.

BETTER HALF

The origin of the modern spouse's humble introduction, "my better half," originates with a tale out of the ancient Middle East. The story tells of a Bedouin who had offended his prince and the subject's faithful wife, who pleaded for her husband's life.

"O, great Prince, the blasphemy is horrible. I confess. But it is not my whole husband who has thus rendered himself guilty toward Thee."

"Not thy whole husband?" the Prince replied.

"Nay," she continued, "it is but half, the half of him that has committed the insult; for am I not the other half, I who have never offended thee? Now the guilty half places itself under the protection of the innocent half and the latter cannot suffer the former to be punished."

From this ancient concept of a man and woman being merged into one by marriage comes the modern phrase, "better half."

MAKING ENDS MEET

"Making ends meet" is often associated with an ability to stay afloat financially. Who would have thought that a phrase that now applies to the continual economic struggles of common folks would have evolved from the ordeal connected with obtaining the funds necessary to dress a well-heeled lady properly?

To be dressed properly, the lady of fashion in the eighteenth and nineteenth centuries often required assistance in pulling together the two ends of her corset and buckling it when both ends met. Her dress would not hang properly unless a helper, generally her maligned husband, had hooked together numerous latches, all of which required tedious and cautious pulling to "make the ends meet." Even a lady's shoes and galoshes of yesteryear were equipped with leather thongs, the ends of which had to be brought together before they could be buckled.

At first the expression referred simply to the physical ordeal accompanying a lady's dressing. As the cost of her ensemble increased and the difficulty in putting it together diminished, "making ends meet" came to refer to the financial ordeal connected with gathering the funds necessary to dress a lady properly.

FLY OFF THE HANDLE

This phrase originated in the backwoods of antebellum America when wood chopping was a necessity and had to be done by hand with an ax. Each ax had a long, smooth handle, and unless the woodsman held the handle tightly at all times, the ax would "fly off the handle." From this frequent experience, colonial woodsmen came to call outbursts of bad temper "flying off the handle."

CUT AND DRIED

When something is simple or easy to explain, we say that it's "cut and dried." For this expression, we are once again indebted to the lumber trade. Wood, among lumbermen, is not lumber until it has gone through two processes. First it is cut. Then it is dried. Only then is it lumber, ready for sale and use.

CLARK'S CREDO

I'm smart and talented, and I never say "never."

I'm wanted, important, lovable, and capable, and I can succeed.

I have pride, class, flexibility, grace, discipline, and balance.

I'm a good athlete, I love music, and I get good grades in school.

I never say "I can't"—I always say "I can, and I will."

If I fall down or fail, I just get back up and go again.

If I spill or make a mistake, I learn why, clean it up, and say, "No big deal."

I treat others as I want to be treated.

I always tell the truth and play by the rules.

I dream mighty dreams. If I don't dream, how can I make a dream come true?

I love God and will do the right thing simply because it's the right thing to do.

Therefore, I leave no regrets by always leaving my family, friends, job, neighborhood, country, and world in better shape than I found them. I'm somebody very special. No one can ever take my place. Whenever I leave, everybody says, "I like me best when I'm with you. I want to see you again."

QUOTES

GEORGE CARLIN

The paradox of our time in history is that we have taller buildings but shorter tempers; wider freeways but narrower viewpoints. We spend more but have less; we buy more but enjoy less. We have bigger houses and smaller families; more conveniences but less time. We have more degrees but less sense; more knowledge but less judgment. We've learned how to make a living but not a life; we've added years to life not life to years. We've been all the way to the moon and back but have trouble crossing the street to meet a new neighbor. We conquered outer space but not inner space. We've done larger things but not better things.

GENERAL J.F.C. FULLER

We shall teach each other. First, because we have a vast amount of experience behind us. Second, it is only through free criticism of each other's ideas that truth can be thrashed out. No one is going to compel you to work, for the simple reason that a man who requires to be driven is not worth the driving. Thus, you will become your own student and until you learn how to teach yourself, you will never be taught by others.

CHUANG TZU

Do not make easy hard. Wisdom is understandable. Be clear in all teachings. You cannot speak of ocean to a well frog, the creature of a narrower sphere. You cannot speak of ice to a summer insect, the creature of a season.

* * *

ALBERT EINSTEIN

Learning is its own exceeding great reward. And stay the course, for great spirits have always encountered violent opposition from mediocre minds. The mind once stretched can never return to its original dimensions.

ERIC HOFFER

In times of change learners inherit the earth, while the learned find themselves beautifully equipped to deal with a world that no longer exists

* ✶ *

MARCUS AURELIUS

Today is yesterday's pupil. To disdain today (it is the first day of the rest of your life) is to prove that yesterday has been misunderstood. Remember, the only life which a man can lose is that which he is living at the moment.

ELEANOR ROOSEVELT

Do one thing each and every day that scares you.

* * *

GILBERT ARLAND

When an archer misses the mark he turns and looks for the fault within himself. Failure to hit the bull's-eye is never the fault of the target. To improve your aim, improve yourself.

ALAN HARRINGTON

We are all, it seems, saving ourselves for the senior prom. But many of us forget that somewhere along the way we must learn to dance.

* * *

CARMEN SNOW

The world needs dreamers and the world needs doers, but above all the world needs dreamers who do.

JOHN F. KENNEDY

I think this is the most extraordinary collection of talent and human knowledge that has ever been gathered together at the White House, with the possible exception of when Thomas Jefferson dined alone.

* * *

RALPH WALDO EMERSON

If you find life is empty, try putting something into it. Kindness is the language the deaf can hear and the blind can see. You cannot do a kindness too soon because you never know how soon it will be too late.

WILLIAM JAMES

The deadliest enemies of nations are not their foreign foes; they always dwell within their borders. And from these internal enemies civilization is always in need of being saved. The nation blessed above all nations is she in whom the civic genius of the people does the saving day-to-day, by acts without external picturesqueness; by speaking, writing, voting reasonably; by smiting corruption swiftly; by good temper between parties; by the people knowing true men when they see them, and preferring them as leaders to rabid partisans or empty quacks.

WILLIAM HAZLITT

To think justly, we must understand what others mean; to know the value of our thoughts, we must try their effect on other minds. To effectively communicate, we must connect beyond the ears, listen heart to heart, and perfect the art of persuasion.

⁎ ⁎ ⁎

ARISTOTLE

What is a friend? A single soul dwelling in two bodies.

WILLIAM GEORGE JORDAN

The man who has a certain belief and fears to discuss it, lest it may be proved wrong, is not loyal to his beliefs; he has but a coward's faithfulness to his prejudices. If he were a lover of truth, he would be willing at any moment to surrender his belief for a higher, better, and truer faith. When you want to believe in something, you also have to believe in everything that's necessary for believing in it.

DONALD "DOC" SANSOM

The first wealth is health. A sound mind in a sound body, a short but full description of a happy state in this world.

* * *

THOMAS JEFFERSON

Too old to plant trees for my own gratification, I shall do it for my posterity.

WINSTON CHURCHILL

Success is the ability to go from one failure to another with no loss of enthusiasm.

* * *

IRVING BERLIN

The toughest thing about success is that you've got to keep on being a success.

MICHEL DE MONTAIGNE

We should take care not to make the intellect our God; it has, of course, powerful muscles, but no personality. The mind has great influence over the body and is a dangerous weapon, if he knows not discretely how to use it.

* * *

HERMAN MELVILLE

We cannot live for ourselves alone. Our lives are connected by a thousand invisible threads, and along these sympathetic fibers, our actions run as causes and return to us as desired results.

ROBERT PEDERSEN

Too often we forget that you can surgically remove the stripes from a tiger, and it's still a tiger. A geographic relocation doesn't change much. No matter where you go, there you are.

* * *

JOHANN WOLFGANG VON GOETHE

Behavior is a mirror in which everyone displays his own image. Conduct is three-fourths of our life and its largest concern.

CALVIN COOLIDGE

Nothing in the world can take the place of persistence. Talent will not; nothing is more common than unsuccessful men with talent. Genius will not; unrewarded genius is almost a proverb. Education will not; the world is full of educated derelicts. Persistence and determination alone are omnipotent. The slogan "Press on" has solved and always will solve the challenges of the human race.

0 26575 70497 6